# If God Is a Woman,
# Who Am I?

# *If God Is a Woman, Who Am I?*

POEMS AND STORIES

Written by

Danna Schweitzer

Copyright © 2009 by Danna Schweitzer.
Illustrated by Mickey Phillips
Photos by Danna Schweitzer

ISBN:        Softcover         978-1-4415-0874-4

All rights reserved. No part of this book may be reproduced or transmitted in any form or by any means, electronic or mechanical, including photocopying, recording, or by any information storage and retrieval system, without permission in writing from the copyright owner.

This book was printed in the United States of America.

**To order additional copies of this book, contact:**
Xlibris Corporation
1-888-795-4274
www.Xlibris.com
Orders@Xlibris.com
58854

# Contents

Acknowledgements .................................................................... 7

Life Lived .................................................................................. 9
If God Is a Woman, Who Am I? ............................................ 11
If God is a woman then who am I ........................................ 21
Be Present to the Moment ..................................................... 23
Light in the Desert ................................................................. 24
Growing In To God ................................................................ 37
Pondering a Vocation ............................................................ 38
Evil ........................................................................................... 40
The Box .................................................................................... 41
Mother Love ............................................................................ 43
It is that time of year ............................................................. 45
Self Portrait ............................................................................. 46

Bibliography ........................................................................... 47

# Acknowledgements

No creative work, whether fact or fiction, occurs in a vacuum. The time and space to create must be granted to you by friends and family. Therefore, I must thank my husband Rick and our children Mickey, Chris, John, Rodney, Tracy, Cathy, David, and Tina. Inspiration comes covered in smiles and tears.

The Sisters of Benedict at Red Plains Monastery, Jan, Benedicta, Marie, Joanne, Melissa, Eunice, and Miriam for their many prayers and friendship. My instructors at Aquinas Institute of Theology, Saint Louis University for continued encouragement to write and share as I work through the Master of Arts Pastoral Ministry program. Sister Diane Koorie, guide and mentor for many years as I travel through the maze of education. Mary Diane, my own spiritual director and guide as you listen and notice.

Thanks to my parents Dan and Geraldine Salmon, the first true seekers I ever knew. Being who they were, individually and alone, started me on the journey to who I am today. Thanks also to Mike, Paddy, Kathy, and Sally who keep me grounded and never fail to remind me of who I really am when it comes time to clean house. We are brothers and sisters forever.

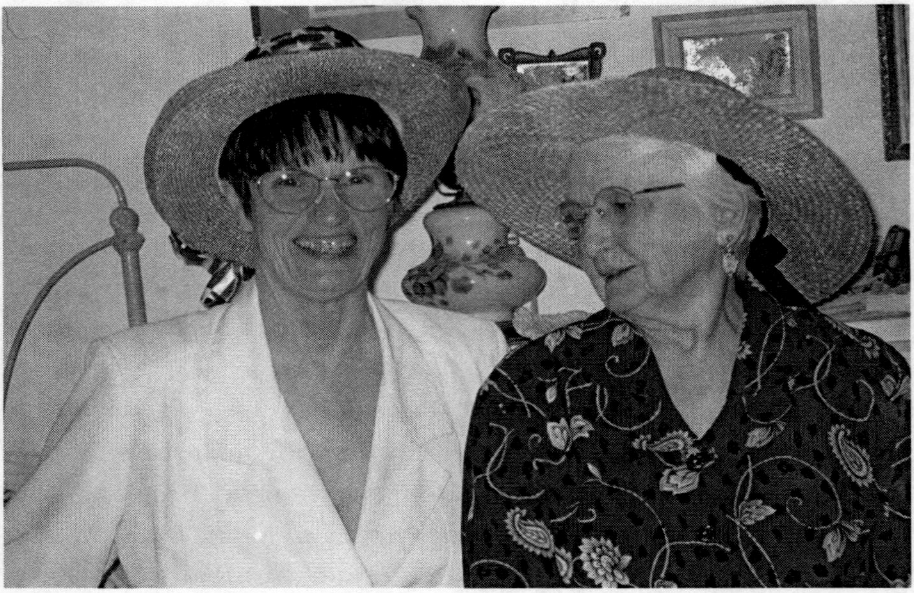

# Life Lived

I stopped today and watched apple blossoms
Blown to earth on dry warm winds
The scurry of life melts
I am aware of—pride
Pride of place in the world
I do not own this
I am but steward to the life God has given me
A life meant to be lived
More than pondered over

# If God Is a Woman, Who Am I?

California's Napa valley is usually a pleasant place to drive especially along a winding country road in a top down convertible in early spring. The rest of the nation is still locked in snow and cold rain while I feel warm air and smell fragrant early blooms. This is when it is easy to love God. Of course, I'm not really here for a joy ride. I come on a mission, a retreat to the Passionist Fathers monastery seeking discernment. What do I want to be when I grow up?

Considering my age, that is a rhetorical question. For many people, the age of 60 is a full lifetime. More specifically, I am on a quest to understand why I continue to pursue an education. I am a wife, a mother of grown children, and a religious education teacher at my church. I am also a student seeking a Master of Arts degree in Pastoral Ministry. Rarely has a week gone by that someone does not ask me "So what are you going to do with your degree? Women in the Catholic Church can't do much, can they?" I usually just laugh and change the subject.

My gaze shifts and I catch the sight of the leather bound book lying in the seat next to me. My Grandmother is an odd duck, nearly 100 years old and still trying to tell everybody around her what to do. I had stopped to visit her at the nursing home on my way to the retreat house and she gives me this 'book'. I tried to tell her that I needed no gifts, but she insisted and I really don't know her well enough to argue. She is my mother's mother, my real mother, that is. You see, I lost Mom to cancer when I was only seven and Dad had remarried. Louise was a great step mom but we had generally lost touch with the Reyes side of the family. Nothing intentional, just a drifting away that was never really reconciled until I started writing about ten years ago, first to an uncle and then to Grandmother.

I did get to learn something of that family's journey. Because they are generally Hispanic in appearance, I had assumed that they came to the United States from Mexico like many of the families in California. In our correspondence, I found that we originally came from Spain or a place that Grandmother called Castilano. The founding family left sometime after Spain became a united country under Emperor Charles V and spent a couple of generations traveling without going through Mexico, until they reached this lovely part of the world.

My thoughts dissolve back to the present as I arrive at the monastery. A quiet pristine place ideal for contemplation, where I am ushered to a room, introduced to a director, and given the schedule for prayer and meeting times. The chapel is very beautiful and the monks sing like angels. Supper is very good, not what some might expect if our idea of monastery life is austerity and plain living. Then to the quiet of my room with no television and no telephone, I turn to books. The most interesting book is the gift from Grandmother.

Hand sewn and leather covered, the pages are very old and written in ink. Amazingly, they do not crumble away as I carefully turn them. The writing is odd and yet I can see some familiar words. The book is written primarily in Spanish, a very old form of Spanish. Now I am quite grateful for the hours I spent in college trying to force this 'foreign' language into my head. Even though my mother's family looks Spanish, they do not speak it in any form. As far as I know, they have no ties with any country other than this one but that also explains why Grandmother was so mysterious about what was in the book.

She had shared with me that the book was a diary written by a priest, a distant family member. Her belief was that it contained instructions on how to be a good priest. No family member had known enough Spanish to translate it in her childhood but it had been dutifully passed to her by a great uncle who had received it from his mother with the instruction to pass it to any family member who had chosen to follow a vocation. It would guide them as they accepted the ordained life. She explained that as no member of our family had done so in two generations, she had no choice but to pass it on to the 'next best thing'. It was not a compliment and I certainly did not feel honored.

I settle in and begin to translate what words I can. There are sentence fragments and words that I cannot decipher. The Spanish is old and the use of some verbs is strange compared to what I remember. Through the first three pages, I cannot find any evidence of a name but the date 19 March 1546 is very clear. An ancient document indeed, intriguing but it will have to wait for morning.

I rise with the sun and head for the chapel first thing. Morning Prayer is beautiful and quick enough followed by an even faster breakfast. I waste little time finding the library and am delighted to locate not only a Spanish dictionary and history book but also a very old Spanish/English dictionary to help me with the obscure words. The next stop is my Spiritual director Fr. Morales, a kindly retired priest who admits to spending his days puttering in the rose garden and visiting with the directees who come his way. I share with him my Grandmothers gift and he is amazed.

"Oh, my dear, this is a treasure. Is it a diary? Could it be from the time of the Council of Trento?" He is nearly breathless as he tenderly holds the book in his weathered hands.

"Well, I'm not really sure", I answer, "but I would like the opportunity to work on translating as much of this as I can while I'm here. Would that be alright?"

"Well, of course" he smiles, "do you feel called to do this work?"

I answer in the affirmative relieved to have found a 'job' for my retreat. It will give me structure and focus. Fr. Morales seems genuinely pleased that I have shared my 'gift' with him and we set another time for tomorrow. I am warned not to miss my prayer times or meals in pursuit of 'the mystery', as he comes to call the book.

I begin the work in my room at a small writing desk but quickly enough slip out into the sunshine and a large picnic table under a tree within sight of my door. I translate the words one by one at first using a pad and pencil. Eventually moving to connected statements and sentences. After noon prayer and lunch, I look at my translation in total and try to read the first few entries. It is a diary written by a Trinidad de Roias, clerk or scribe to Francisco de Toledo. He appears to be a young man who has come with his boss to a meeting of some sort. There are mentions of discussions about Scripture and the desire of the Church legates. On page 7, an entry clearly announces the death of Martin Luther. There is little sadness from the author but he seems to share some sympathy for the 'followers of Luther who have traveled to Trento to have a voice at the council'. I stare at the page as a shudder runs through my body. Can I believe my eyes? Could the translation be correct? Is this a diary of a person who possibly attended the Council of Trent? This is too unbelievable. I bend to my task and the day flies.

Each morning I meet with Fr. Morales and share the knowledge I have gleaned from the pages of the little buckskin book. I am excited to have this window on the past but a part of my feeling is the possibility that some how I may be related to this author. Fr. Morales shares with me his excitement for he had been privileged to attend a few of the sessions of Vatican Council II in the early 1960's.

The diary shares with us about the Council and especially the contention and division experienced between many of the bishops and the representatives of Luther. Each country's clergy members seem more attached to the king or emperor than to the pope. I am reminded that these bishops were appointed and possibly paid by the local king or crown prince and not by the Bishop of Rome. Although there is agreement that the church needs reform, there is a great difference of opinion as to how this will take place. Word comes every few days from Emperor Charles and reports are sent back daily to his Excellency.

In the first sessions the subject was the Scriptures. In treating the canon of Scripture they declare the Vulgate to be the authentic text for sermons, teaching, and disputations. At the request of the Spanish Emperor the general congregation took up the discussion of original sin and its cancellation by baptism. Our young diarist is very proud to have been a member of the group able to bring this important matter before the council. It is noted that the question of the Immaculate Conception of the Virgin was brought forward, but the majority of the members finally decided not to give any decision.

Fr. Morales is delighted at this mention of the Immaculate Conception. He reminds me that this subject was taken up by a later Pope, Pius IX, and was the subject of one of the few 'ex cathedra' statements ever made. We chuckle over the sentence, which states that the Latin Vulgate Bible is the only one recognized by God. This also changed before Vatican Council II and we agree that the People of God are the better for it.

The little book is filled with all the sights and sounds surrounding the council even more than the goings on inside. Young Trinidad writes of the awful fighting between the legates and the bishops both inside and outside the chambers where the council is held. This is scandalous to him and he begs God's mercy for the men he sees as his example and his mentor. "How am I to live the Gospel as a servant of the Lord if this is what I see before me?" It would appear that Trini is speaking of his own vocation to the priesthood. Of course, until this time there were still some areas in Europe where children were sent away to join religious groups and there may or may not have been much schooling involved before vows were taken.

An entry dated in March of 1547 states that the legates to the council have left for Bologna but the Spanish representatives and bishops remain in Trent at the order of the Emperor. Trinidad is fearful that the work of reform will be undone. The next entry is nearly ten months later and written in Poza where he has gone to spend some time with his parents before he is called back to the council. He continues to prepare letters and documents for the church and government officials as needed. He writes now of a friend named Cruz. They seem to be quite close although perhaps this is a young woman. This is one of those names that can be either male or female.

The next entry in the book is 1552 and written in a different hand. Now the diarist is writing about Trinidad. We learn that along with the knowledge of writing he is also a very gifted speaker. There is a gathering where Trini is called to speak and proclaim the greatness of the Lord. So effective was the confession that nearly 500 men and women were retuned to the Roman church from Islam that day. Fr. Morales is enthusiastic but also a little dismayed.

"What do suppose happened to the Council," he asked. "Of course, if memory serves me well it was suspended sometime that year." He wondered aloud if the writer might not be the spouse of Trinidad de Roias. I offered that if this was a priest then the relationship might not have gone well which would be sad indeed.

It is not very many pages before the new writer in the journal is discovered; it is Cruz Perez. We feel we have found a possible spouse. The work of Trinidad and Cruz is now centered on their work in a church in Zamora. Cruz and Trinidad work with the poor and the widows finding them food and shelter. Trini is now censured from speaking and it is most heartbreaking for both of them. Perhaps he did not become a priest.

"How do you feel about this?" Fr. Morales asks. "What might God be telling them in this?" This is a hard question. Is it possible that God is not saying anything but that men for some unknown reason have made a decision that affects this life? On the other hand, perhaps it is the results of an institution (the church) living in this historical era when they are beginning to require uniformity from the clergy.

If this had happened to me—what am I saying, on some level this is happening to me? True, I have never spoken before congregations and brought souls to the church as this young man did but . . .

Fr. Morales interrupts my thought, "Are you sure about that? Did you not tell me that you taught in your RCIA program? Well, what is that if not bringing souls to the Lord?" Now I begin to understand and allow my own feelings to filter into the story of this young possible relative. How hurtful to have believed that God called him to a ministry only to be turned away by the institution you view as a conduit to that same God. Yet, he and his friend continue to do the work required of them by the gospel. Perhaps this is a little bit like me also.

The next entries begin in 1559 in Valladolid. The parents of Trinidad, Don Luigi and Donna Maria de Roias have been accused of joining the Lutheran church, which has been forbidden by the Catholic Church in Spain. They have been arrested and will be brought to trial in the morning. It is the 'Auto de Fey' the Spanish Inquisition. The writer prays desperately that the parents will be spared, that the inquisitors will see that these two people are innocent of any such accusation.

Fr. Morales reflects, "What difference would it make if these were your ancestors and they had been guilty or, worse yet, innocently murdered by this inquisition? Would it change your feelings about the Church?" This is a difficult question. In my work in RCIA, I have met individuals who felt anger or resentment over some thing in their past. Sometimes is has been clear even to me that the Church owed them an apology but nothing official would be forthcoming. Could I forgive this institution? Will Trini and Cruz forgive?

The next date is nearly a month later. The entire family has been rescued from Spain and placed on a ship bound for the new world. There are praises to God and the Virgin thanking them for safe passage from the inquisitor. The next lines are shocking. The diarist has enumerated the family members. There are the parents Don Luigi and Donna Maria de Roias, Cruz and Trinidad Perez, Juan, Cruz, and Maria. I look again, count, and retranslate. To my amazement, I find that Trinidad de Roias Perez is a woman, now married to Cruz Perez and the mother of three. Our blessed Trini was a young girl who longed to be a priest. In the history book I read that up until the end of the Medieval Period, persons were sometimes elected by their communities for possible candidacy for ordination. For a woman to have been chosen was possibly remote by this time but evidently Ms Trinidad possessed many of the gifts required in the priestly office. After all, she had been chosen as scribe to accompany the Emperor's representative at one of the most important gatherings of that decade.

I turn two more pages of text and see a list of names beginning with Cruz and Trinidad, beneath them names and years inscribed for eight persons. The third name down, Maria is transposed below the list and attached to it is Don Carlos followed by six more names and dates. It is a genealogy of this family picking out the name of the oldest daughter in each set. A line is drawn connecting these eldest women together so that they flow from one generation to the next for a total of twelve generations. The line ends at my Grandmothers name. Below her are dutifully written my mothers name along with her two brothers—all of whom are now deceased. I realize that my name should follow along with the name of my eldest daughter.

I take the diary to Fr. Morales and he asks me to translate the last pages. It is a difficult task. While I am translating, he asks questions of me.

"You can see that your family has survived and along with it the Catholic Church, and is it the same Church?"

It is not, at least not the Church created at Trent and yet much of what was decided in the sixteenth century was necessary to stop the abuses that were being created by the men who were in control. Of course, this is an institution, which exists within history, and the abuses were extensions of the way men and women were treated in most areas of life. The changes created by Popes and Councils down through the history of humanity have brought us a little closer to the true teaching of Jesus Christ each time.

Fr. Morales began to speak softly, "You know, I remember how is was in those days of Pope John and then Pope Paul, we were trying so to bring some growing Spirit that we all felt back into the Church. There were things that were agreed upon that were implemented rather quickly and some things that still wait. Perhaps it was not the right time. The words were written but there were consequences that the Church Fathers had not foreseen. The large numbers who chose to leave rather than change and the small schisms created when some could neither leave nor change.

I had a brother priest who chose to leave and I have missed him every day since then."

The translation was finished and I read it to my Spiritual Director. It was a message for those who would come after, to the generations of women symbolized by the names on the final pages. The Grandmother wrote, "We are a faith filled people of God, a God who has no gender. Pray for us my daughters. Know that this God and this once living Son love us and will never abandon those who believe. One day I pray that my call to be ordained will find fruition in a woman who will come after me. The times must change and I believe that they will. We embark on a great adventure secure in the love of the one God and those who follow the call."

In the silence that followed Fr. Morales mused, "Some decades ago it was proposed that perhaps God was a woman. This intrigued many and I know there have been books and plays written which entertain this theology. At first I thought it would change nothing but as I have lived out my life I realize that it does affect how I see myself as a man."

I offered that I had never wanted to be a priest but on considering the diary perhaps that is because I never knew, I could be. I believe that God is bringing us to right thinking as a community. We are asked to live life in the way of Jesus with justice for all, but we as community can move forward no faster than the least accepting of us. The Church and human history have changed and will continue to change through the rest of God's time. Only God will be always the same.

"And what will you say when asked what you will do with your degree, my dear", said Fr. Morales.

I would say that like my ancestors, I will teach and, if God wills it, I will bring souls to Jesus Christ and the fullness of the Church that I know.

"You are an orator of great faith and power. You have in your hands a great spiritual guide writ in a book" Fr. Morales blessed me and we prayed together. I lifted my bag and headed for my car with 'my' diary firmly in hand.

Driving back down the winding valley road, I pondered my encounter. I needed to know this history and with this priest as guide, I could make sense of it. Then it came to me—if God is a woman, who am I? At first, it did not sink in but so much in the history of humanity has appeared to be gender based. If we are all created in the image of God and the Body of Christ, the Son, is the Church then it does affect who I am.

The sun begins to sink below the horizon and a great calm washes over me. I will be different, perhaps better, from this time to whatever comes next.

# If God is a woman then who am I

The cloth of my faith has been woven
Over days and weeks and years have I have spun
Carefully crafting the tapestry of knowledge
The time to gather it in has begun

If God is a woman, then who am I

Does this last thread change the weaving?
Or can this bring the cloth to its end
The last thread is sent and tamped down
Is there more that Wisdom will send

If God is woman then who am I?

Or does this change me at all
I wish to cry "no, I shall not change", and yet
I know that all is relative and connected
With all that exists now and before

I am I
Who am
Who once was
Perhaps one day will be

If God is a woman I will change
And become more
Than I might have been

But God is neither man nor woman
And the weave of my cloth is true
I must wrap this tapestry round me
And wait for Wisdom too.

# Be Present to the Moment

A thousand times I may walk the labyrinth and still not see your face.

A hundred times I may kneel in prayer and still not feel your grace.

No magic or potion or talisman draws me close to God, I fear

Only silence and waiting as an open heart listens for the voice so clear.

Growing up, growing old, and changing places, changing times.

Closer to the heartbeat

# Light in the Desert

Bumping along a desert 'road' in a canvas-topped jeep has never been my idea of a fun thing to do, but it was the quickest way to travel. The air was hot even though we were 'flying low' at 50 kilometers per hour and the sun was not quite up. Miserable was the only word I could think of as I slouched down in an attempt to rest. As an archaeologist, being in the desert on a dig is the joy of my life, but this part of the trip was definitely not part of that joy.

My two colleagues and I had been on a project in North Africa for the better part of a month when we began to experience tremblers. That little shaky thing the earth does when it is trying to adjust its' outer shell. An old professor of mine at the University said it was Mother Nature 'shifting her petticoat'. Anyway, we did not make much of it until late one night when we got an emergency radio call to go to a nearby settlement to help with a rescue. It was not a town we were going to, just a location; but it seems some people there had become trapped in an old cave. This part of the world may look like a giant sand pile but in reality, it is littered with caves and gullies, the sand often rests on top with a network of boulders in place between the topsoil and the strata of soil lower down. If the boulders shift, the sand can collapse and change the whole terrain along with burying any items on top.

I still was not convinced that we three needed to suspend our work but I was not in charge, Janine Davis, our department head held that position and agreed to our mission.

"Be careful about your griping," She said, "when it comes to rescues, you never know who God will pick."

We were closer than any authorities in the area were and we did have some medical supplies as well as modern communication equipment.

The jeep lurched to a stop and I opened my eyes to a rather large group of people in cream-colored robes standing around a pile of rocks on a hillside. About half way up there were swarms of people clawing at a particular spot in the rubble.

"The tremblers must have closed in a cave here," Janine announced. "Frank, you radio the conditions so they know what kind of equipment to send. You can wake up and follow me and stop rolling your eyes." Janine loved to be in charge.

The crowd began to gather around, speaking, and motioning to the mound, so many voices, some in a language I did not recognize. Suddenly a small person wriggled to the front and spoke in very clear English "You American?"

"Yes, and we are here to help," Janine said.

"Follow please" the person turned out to be a young woman in her twenties. She rushed us forward through the throng explaining along the way that there was a cave, which was inhabited by a person referred to as the Ancient One who, along with a band of followers had lived in this desert for as long as she could remember. Yesterday there had been an earthquake and the entrance to the cave had been closed. Frank, the third member of our team began to relay the story to the Red Cross operator he had reached in the closest major city. As we walked, we heard the operator announce that a sand storm had brewed up between them and us so any rescue effort would be delayed but we were asked to go ahead with what we could.

Janine and I began to pull up rocks and rubble in the spots being worked by the natives. Janine ordered, "You take the south end and I'll help over here. Just be careful where the ground flattens out the cave could be underneath us."

Just because she's the head of the team and a geologist does not mean that I'm an idiot. I think I know how the desert plays with you. The little interpreter and I set to work, when another tremble hit. I stood still and waited. Suddenly, the ground beneath me gave way and I found myself tumbling head over tail into the dark. I closed my eyes and tried to cover my head from the falling debris. I felt the sand and rocks wrapping around me and I was very conscious of fearing that I would be buried alive. Then the shaking stopped. I held my breath for a second and then opened my eyes. I could see nothing. Either I had fallen into a cave and the earth had covered me, as Janine said, or I had gone blind. At least I was still breathing and I felt no pressure on my chest although I did feel that my legs and the left side of my body were being held captive. No pain meant I had spinal injuries or I was just encased in debris either way I was still alive. "Hello" I called softly, "anybody out there".

I felt as though I was in a larger space. My right hand and arm were free so I tried feeling for something but found nothing but the dark. No walls, no rocks, no person, just empty space. I started trying to peal the rocks and sand from my body. Suddenly a voice called out, "Ouch". I stopped and listened.

"Is anybody there?" I said.

"Yes," the answer came. "I'm here but I think I'm trapped." It was the little interpreter. I was suddenly grateful for another voice.

"Well, be careful and try not to shift too much," I instructed, "I can't see where we are but we may be in a cave or a clear space. Can you see anything?"

"No," she said and began to whimper. The crying was soft but distinct, now I had more than just me to worry about. We must be in an open area but for how long? They would be clawing away to reach us but there was no way of knowing how much air we had or whether another tremor would crush us where we were. This was fear; I tried desperately to think of something to distract us both. Then there was another sound, it was a voice humming at first, then sounds that might have been words began. Was the little interpreter singing?

"Hey, is that a song you are trying to sing?" I tried to tease.

"No, not me," she sounded even more frightened.

The voice grew slightly louder. The tune began to sound slightly familiar.

> 'Pererin wyf mewn anial dir,
> Yn crwydro yma a thraw;'

"H-h-hello?" my little trapped friend spoke. "Ancient One?"

The words and accent changed but the melody and voice remained the same.

> 'Genade onbeskryflik groot
> Het U aan my bewys'

Now I recognized it, the voice was singing 'Amazing Grace' in Afrikaans. The interpreter recognized it too. She began to talk in a hushed and reverent voice. I had always been unsuccessful at learning languages so I relied on interpreters but one cannot spend a great deal of time in another country without picking up bits. I thought she was asking for prayers. I wondered if the rockslide had injured the old man. The voice was soothing and helped to calm my fears. This was stupid, the guy is nearly buried alive and he starts singing. There is no accounting for these religious kooks.

The singing had stopped so I felt impelled to ask a few questions of my fellow cave dwellers.

"Hey," I said, "can you ask him if he can see anything and by the way, what is your name?"

Her voice came back like a smile, "Okay, my name is Ninjig, it means tall one in my language." She giggled at the irony. Then I heard her saying things to the other voice and that new voice answering. The conversation went on for several minutes before she got back to me. "The Ancient One says there is no light so our eyes cannot work for us. We must use our voices and our hearts to communicate."

"Oh great," I thought to myself, "stuck in the dark with a freaking old man and a mislabeled dwarf. This is how my life will end." I wondered about my life as their conversation continued. I had never been religious or attended any church. I remembered a few hard fought discussions about the existence of God in my undergrad years but it was all an unnecessary mystery to me.

"Hey, American," Ninjig's voice broke into my thoughts. "The Ancient One wishes to know your name. She says you can talk to him straight because he can understand the language she just can't say it very good." It was a little broken but I sure understood.

"Okay," I started "my name is Chris. I'm an archaeologist from the United States. I came here to help you get out of the predicament you are in now. My friends and I have come to help you." The voice answered in a language I still could not put my finger on then Ninjig spoke, "She says you were send to him by God the Only One, to save your soul."

"Whatever," I thought, "if it pleases the old man let it be." The voices went back and forth for a minute. Then I had to speak up, immortal souls or not we were in a very tight spot and needed to have a plan.

"Hey, you two," I said in as commanding a voice as I could muster, "we need to evaluate our situation here. Obviously, we are alive now but the truth is that this whole hillside could go at any second so we need to be trying to dig our way out from inside while the folks up top are trying to work their way down. I am not in any pain so I think I'm okay but my left side and lower torso are embedded in debris. How are the both of you?"

Ninjig answered, "I'm pretty good. I got both arms free but my left one is hurting a lot. There is something holding my feet down but I feel okay. The Ancient One only says she is where God needs him to be. He don't say anything is bad for her."

"Well," I said, "Let's start trying to unearth ourselves. I would suggest that we just sort of move things slowly so we don't disturb the rocks above us or hit one another with anything. Work slowly to conserve energy and air. No telling how long we may be here."

Slowly I began to hear the sound of stones being moved as I moved a few of my own. It felt good to release each bit and portion of my body. Then I noticed a glow, it was my own arm. My watch was faintly glowing in the dark from the energy it had drawn from the sun, dust covered everything so the glow was quite dim. This was great, at least I had some way of calculating time and now I knew I was not blind.

Within a short while, the Old Guy began to sing again, this time a melody I did not recognize. First he hummed and then later added words of some language I did not understand and yet it was comforting. In any other situation, I would be irritated that the Old Thing was not coming across with his condition or doing any more than singing. If he was free, he could be helping us free ourselves. My fears began to work on me and I started moving the stones faster and faster. Soon my left arm was free but I was covered in sweat. I had no idea how far down we actually were but the singing had ended so I decided to pick up the conversation.

"Hey, Ninjig," I asked "does he know how far down we are in this cave?"

The voice answered and in the next moment, she began to interpret. "The Ancient One says we are near the old entrance before the earth shook. It has been covered twice but the people keep pulling the rocks away. The cave slopes down and away very far back so there is much room if we were free to move."

That was good news. If the cave is large then we may be in a place with plenty of air and if we could just break loose from the rocks around us, we could move farther back away from the weaker formations at the entrance.

"Hey, Chris," Ninjig's voice came, "the Ancient One wishes to know how you believe in God."

"Uh, I don't know," this was awkward. "I never thought about it much. I don't think this is the time to worry about philosophy."

"On the contrary," Ninjig interpreted, "he says this is the most perfect time to reflect on life and why we are here in this place at this time."

Now I was irritated. "Just tell him to start singing"

I worked a few more stones before I noticed that there was no singing, in fact, there was no noise at all coming from either one of them. "Hey, Ninjig," I said, "Are you okay? Where's the music? Ninjig?" Silence enveloped me. I cried out a few more times but then, eventually I must have fallen asleep. I had leaned my head against the cool stone and felt the tiredness creep into my body.

Suddenly, I was jerked awake by the sound of something scratching at the stone near my hand. The glow from my watch showed a pair of insects preparing to investigate my finger. I flipped them away and checked the time. It was at least seven hours since I had last checked it. I decided to try again. "Ninjig?" I spoke clearly "Ancient One?"

The voice floated through the dark, "Ah Chris, you have awake. Ninjig is rest more." I recognized the tenor of the voice and knew it was the old guy. He knew more of the language than he let on before I fell asleep.

Then my friend spoke. "I'm here, Ancient One. My arm is very painful now. Please can you help?"

"Stretch out your arm if you can for I am trap also." The voice continued in the strange language then ended in words I had heard before—"in Jesus name." I was surprised. I always thought of people around here as being Muslim, but perhaps these were members of some Christian group that lived in the desert to avoid confrontation. It did not matter; the thing now was about getting out alive. I felt a bit embarrassed as though I should not be listening to the conversation but I was trapped too.

Next Ninjig's voice floated through the darkness "You okay, Chris? The Ancient One has pray for me and now I feel much better. She can pray for you also."

"Thanks, kid" I answered, "I got too many other things on my mind." I tried to peer into the dark to see the place where the voices came from but the glow from the watch was deteriorating. Still no sounds from above, nothing to indicate they were trying to reach us. I wanted to give up, to say 'the hell with it' and cry like a big old baby but that might frighten the others. How do I do anything stuck in a rockslide in the dark at what was obviously going to become my grave.

I decided to strike up a conversation with Ninjig to distract us and find out some facts about what these people were even doing out here. Ninjig shared with me that she had been to the United States to study medicine several years ago but had chosen to return early when her father died. That accounted for her ability to translate and speak English. She lived with her mother and two younger brothers in a village only half a days walk from the cave.

Ninjig explained that this was the dwelling place of a holy person they referred to as the "Ancient One". Each year for a certain part of the year, he would come and sit in the cave like a hermit, visiting with passersby, forgiving sin, baptizing, and prophesying. The people of her village would seek him out as they traveled through the region, as did many of the nomadic groups who populated this part of the earth. The old one was a Christian, a follower of Jesus Christ of Nazareth, from centuries before. It was said that the Ancient One could not die and would dwell with mankind until the end of the world when Jesus would return.

I continued to pick at the debris around me, wavering between terror at the situation and genuine curiosity at the things this young woman was telling me. My watch light was growing dimmer and the darkness became palpable.

"How is your arm? Are you cured?" The question was meant to be a tease.

"Of course, the prayers of the Ancient One are always answered by God, especially when asked for in the name of Jesus the Christ." Ninjig answered with very disarming confidence.

"So, just who is this Jesus Christ to you?" I was not prepared for the answer I received. The voice of the old man spoke and then Ninjig interpreted.

> Jesus is that once living person
> Person of earth and Son of Man
>
> Jesus is Christ in his death and rising
> Dying and living again in God's light
>
> Jesus is man and Son of the Godhead
> Godhead creator and light to us all
>
> Jesus is the mirror of Yahweh
> Yahweh the lover of humankind

Was this a prayer or a theological statement? Maybe it was both. I had only attended church as a youngster back home. It was Sunday school and a preaching service that said more about God punishing than loving. I had a roommate in college who was into the church thing and tried dragging me along to services but that was a rebellious time for me. Sitting here in a black hole with nothing else to think about I wondered at my decisions.

"Look," I offered "I understand that those are all nice stories, the baby Jesus in a manger and giving up your life for your friends, but be honest, it is just a story. I remember the discussions in college and one person in my dorm said that the followers of Jesus made it up."

The soft voice of the old one intertwined with the singsong meter of Ninjig's recitation

> Perhaps we hear God's call in a wind song
> Perhaps we see God's touch in a tree
> Perhaps we think we do not know God
> But, God is our maker that cannot be
>
> Jesus is the Son of the Father
> Searching for hearts to return to the fold
> If he is false then why do men claim him?
> Claim him as Savior for young and for old
>
> Christ can arrive if we but seek him
> Knock and the door shall be opened for you
> Each generation must ask the same questions
> Search for light that is pure and true

I continued to pick at the rocks around my body as I listened and pondered the words I heard from Ninjig. My glowing watch was dark now but somehow the sound of the two voices with me made the situation livable. It was not that I was not scared but at least I was not alone, my stomach ached with hunger and there had been nothing to drink for at least twenty-four hours. In the darkness I heard something moving toward me, I hoped it was one of them.

Ninjig's voice broke in, "Chris, the Ancient One comes to bring you drink."

Thank God, you might think he could read my mind. Well, probably not. After this many hours in one place, it was a natural move. Who knew he had anything.

"Great, "I answered, "Have you got anything to eat?"

There was no answer but I felt the touch of a hard metal container on my shoulder. I grabbed it and drank not caring much what was in it. I tried not to drink too much wanting to reserve some for the others. The body that brought the flask retreated and I continued to work at the rocks. Then Ninjig announced that she was free and would come to help me.

"Ninjig," I asked softly, "ask him about all that punishment for sin stuff. Does he teach about that? That is what I remember from church. Sin and salvation."

"Ah" the voice spoke with a chuckle "now we interest God's child. Is good"

Once again, Ninjig interpreted:

> Salvation is that which makes us human
> Takes us from darkness and into the light
>
> Moves us from chaos, despair and destruction
> Puts us in place with God as our love
>
> Salvation changes the way that we view things
> Humbles and gladdens our heats and our minds
>
> Makes us a bridge instead of a fencepost
> Gives us a vision of who we can be

We worked on my encasement in silence. Eventually, we heard the sound of a quiet little snore; it was the Ancient One sleeping.

Ninjig and I began to talk very quietly as we worked. She explained that she and her family were followers of the Catholic Church. The Ancient One was thought to be a teacher from a monastery or a commune as he did not offer services like the priests at the church. The village viewed him as a prophet or holy person more attached to God than to any humans. He would read from the same holy book that they all used so she knew he was Christian. The most impressive thing she talked about was the way the ideals taught by the seer changed the way people acted. She told stories of people who were cruel or unkind but who changed after spending time learning from him. She told stories of miraculous healings and people becoming some one new—not just to others but to themselves as well. Live near the desert was harsh and it took the whole community working together to make it livable.

She talked of her time at the college in America where she had expected all things to be wonderful because the people had so much and how she was mistaken. She found the students often to be unkind and uncaring. For all the things they had, they seemed to lack hope. The smallest problem or trouble became a hardship over which they would give up even their own lives. She liked it better here where hope and Christianity truly intertwined with daily living.

Eventually, the rocks were all removed from around me. I was relieved and a little amazed that there were no broken bones or damage that I could locate. I leaned back against my former prison and once again fell asleep.

Suddenly, I was jerked awake by the tapping beside me. It was someone from the outside. Ninjig had fallen asleep beside me and the jolt awakened her. We both sat upright and listened intently.

"Do you hear that?" I whispered.

"Yes, they come for us." She whispered back.

We turned to where the tapping was the loudest and began to claw at the rocks. Suddenly another torrent of rock and sand came spilling in around us. This time we were rolled down into the cave and landed on top of the Ancient One curled up near the side of the cave. Ninjig began to cry. The Ancient One began to sing. It was 'Amazing Grace' again. I guess it was a way to comfort all of us. Then the singing ended and we listened to the tapping at the cave entrance.

As we sat in silence afraid to move for fear of dislodging another landslide, I felt warmth within me. My mind would not focus on the tapping at the rocks. I wanted to know more about what we had been discussing. Another part of me was arguing that it was all silliness; I was just stressed from being trapped in a cave.

"Ancient One" I addressed him directly "how do I know that this is all true? How do I figure this out?"

The voice came through the darkness very close to my face and said without interpretation, "You have begin to ask the questions. This is what is required. You will receive the answer in your heart.

> To each heart a perfect answer
> Perfect to that heart alone
> To one who suffers pain
> He is compassion
> To one who is lost
> He is 'The Way'
> To one who hungers,
> He is life bread
> To one in prison
> He is change
> If you seek him
> He will find you

Suddenly, a light broke through. It was so bright that it hurt my eyes. "Hey down there" It was Frank. "Anybody there?"

We all cried out at once. There were cheers from the crowd above.

"You guys have been down there for three days" Franks face now appeared at the entrance, as the whole became larger "Who all is in there, anyways?"

My eyes began to adjust to the light. I looked about, saw two women, and then looked back at the hole. Rocks were falling but only in small amounts. Then I realized that the holy man was not there.

"Ninjig," I cried, "Where is the Ancient One?"

Surprised, Ninjig motioned "She is here, I too am surprised. But God is not concerned about which kind you are to teach the people."

As we rose to walk to the opening the Ancient One lifted her head and said, "Be careful about your judgments, we never know who God will pick."

# Growing In To God

Chase me down the days into the abyss of time
Give light to the dark and silence the din

Chase me down the days the search for solitude
Has ended once again in the face of God before me

Chase me down the days the way is clear, Lord
The path I seek to you is clean and strong

This clay I am, now dried and re-wet often
Ready to be used

Round and round God holds me
Holds me in the palm of His hand

Not through my effort, not always my wish
God holds me and I am loved

Chase no more for now I wait and listen
Watching for the sign to speak or move or stay

Willing watcher for the Lord in His vineyard
Working for the kingdom which is here

# Pondering a Vocation

Sitting and waiting for her to arrive
Surveying landscape and wondering
"How on earth did I get here?"
The inner voice answers,
"You stopped to listen

God searched for you and you
Stopped to listen and saw the truth".
"But this, this work
Me a Spiritual Director?"
An inward gasp escapes.

When we ask why, God says
Why not?
Have I passed the test?
Have I proven my worth?
"This is the test" God chuckles

A rap at the door
She has arrived and I make welcome
She speaks and I listen
I listen and notice as she speaks
Then it is over

I am in one piece and so is she
Farewells made I turn to journal
It was the softness of the movement
The quiet of the spirit
Feeling the ease and knowing

Here and now
Present time to be looked at
God with us both and then
Spirit of the Lord has touched
Not I but we.

Not my place to judge
Not my place to pick or choose
God is the Director but I must be
That voice for her to hear
Spirit must dwell within me

I am not holy, yet
God has chosen me to be
A voice for one lamb to listen
A model for one child to see
And so I am

For this time and this place

# Evil

Evil creeps up and cracks the door
My anger will not send it away.
It lives in lies that swarm about us
Leading away from the light

Evil slips in to peer through a window
I may not ignore its steady gaze
Glare back like a dog with barred teeth
It blinks and rises to the bait

Evil shrinks back with eyes averted
Shine forth love from your heart
Do not love evil
But only see it as creature held captive.

# The Box

One year ago today my sisters and I met for tea and found our Mother dying, a slow, painful, yet gentle process of the spirit leaving the body. This week I began to find the courage to unpack her collected 'things', to take stock of a life lived. As I touched the ordinary objects and photographs, I began to see the journey of a spirit; her life to be sure, but also mine.

There is the picture she took from an old 'Look' magazine—a painting of a small red-headed girl lying tummy-down in a sea of green leaves and daisy petals staring wide-eyed at the sky. She said it reminded her of me when I was young and so she gave it to me when I had become a mother like her. Later I wrote a small verse, framed it and returned it to her. Now it sits telling me who she thought I was, at least as a child.

Spiritual journeys begin before birth when the spark that God makes us to be is nurtured into this world. There are photos of parties and playtimes, children and babies long since grown to adulthood, pour out, and each one brings a memory. Bits of paper filled with childish scrawl and words of love writ by one who had little knowledge of what it meant beyond the family.

My own spiritual journey reaches beyond this box. I moved away and lived a life she would only know through my words and casual photographs.

The woman who owned the things was a part of my journey. I was indeed a part of hers. God is with both of us as we dance in and out of the light.

My sisters and I have often talked of how 'useless' her cherished objects were and yet it seems that there is a history in what I behold. Will my children find my objects of no value? Or will they tell the story of who I was once I go to join the Creator?

In the end it is the relationships that count. It is the legacy of love you give away that shows who you truly are. I have lived ups and downs and walked away from God, which is the way of human be-ing. Someday I too will have my history placed in a cardboard box and kept for some other soul to 'discover'. I was told by a person far wiser than me that we are all just 'cogs in Gods' wheel of life'. This is true but it is also true that we are more if we choose to be. God has given me opportunities to follow the path through his Son, Jesus Christ. I try to follow that, remembering to give what I receive. Like the picture torn from the magazine. I must accept the love, mark it with a small verse from my heart and return it to the next person. This is the way of an ordinary journey, one that may be stored in a cardboard box.

# Mother Love

When your child dies, they were always too young
It's just wrong that it happens that way
When your child dies, you want to crawl inside someone
Who will make the pain go away?

When your child dies, you lose sight of the sun
Not knowing when it will come back
When your child dies, your heart breaks
And nothing will heal the crack

I wish I could say it will be better one day
Like loosing a lover or friend
But they were none of these and the pain's so hard
It feels like it will never end.

When your child dies and leaves you alone
You turn to the God you know
For his child died so long ago

Heart hurting
I sit before the Lord and ponder your passing

Yet, not your passing
For we all must go on from this life

Perhaps it is your pain filled life
That hurts me most
A little glimmer in history
You danced upon the earth
In agony from mans inhuman acts
You ended it.

I could not stop them
But only stand beside you and weep
I said "I know, I also
Hold my hand and believe in tomorrow"

You are no longer near to love
And yet, I feel you
Heart hurting
As we sit before the Lord

# It *is that time of year*

It is that time of year
When lush, green wheat meets bright, yellow leaf
And brilliant blue skies abound
It is that time of year—but not this year

    It is that time of year
    When distant familiar voices call and plans are made,
    For gathering and giving thanks for bounty.
    It is that time of year—but not this year

        Too much is dry this year
        The quenching rains have not come to give life
        Too much has died this year
        We cannot go on until we cry

Will my tears replace the rain?
    Not this year

## Self Portrait

A seeker I am

    In search of a question

        Guided by a light

            In a fog laden land

The answer will come

    If I can find the question

        The answer will come

           From an open heart

# Bibliography

Sources of inspiration for the story titled *If God is a Woman Who Am I?*

Bonner, Jeremy *the Road to Renewal* Catholic University of America Press Washington D.C. 2008

Cahill, Thomas *Mysteries of the Middle Ages* Nan A Talese Doubleday New York 2006

Duffy, Eamon *Saints & Sinners a History of the Popes* Yale University Press New Haven 2002

O'Malley, John *Trent and All That* Harvard University Press Cambridge, MA 2000

O'Toole, James ed. *Habits of Devotion* Cornell University Press Ithaca New York 2004

Mendham, Joseph M.A. ed. *Memoirs of the Council of Trent* James Duncan London 1834

Prusak, Bernard *the Church Unfinished* Paulist Press New York/Mahwah, NJ 2004

Vidmar, John OP *the Catholic Church Through the Ages* Paulist Press New York/Mahwah NJ 2005

Sources for the story titled *Light in the Desert:*

# Books

Brown, Raymond *an Introduction to New Testament Christology* Paulist Press New York/Mahwah 1994
Cavadini, John and Laura Holt Ed. *Who Do You Say That I Am?* University of Notre Dame Press Notre Dame, Indiana 2004
Kasper, Walter *Jesus the Christ* Paulist Press Mahwah NJ 1977
Johnson, Elizabeth *Consider Jesus* Crossroad New York 2006
Rausch, Thomas P *Who Is Jesus?* Liturgical Press Collegeville, MN 2003
Senior, Donald *Jesus: A Gospel Portrait* Paulist Press New York/Mahwah, NJ 1992

# Other Media

Newton, John *Amazing Grace* 1779 lyrics in Afrikaans and Welsh *http://www.cyberhymnal.org*
Oosdyke, Mary Kay *MAPM T520 Christology* classroom and internet studies 2008